la jolla

Text by Gloria Andújar

Photographs by Jeremiah Sullivan

Andújar Communication Technologies, Inc.
La Jolla, California

Cover design by Caroff/Reiken, New York
Cover photograph by Jeremiah Sullivan, San Diego
Color separations by American Color Corporation, San Diego
Editorial services by SCI-TECH Communication Services, Encinitas
Graphic design, typography and mechanicals by Moog and Associates, Inc., La Jolla
Printing by Toppan Company, Ltd., Tokyo

Published by
Andújar Communication Technologies, Inc.
P.O. Box 2622
La Jolla, California 92038

ISBN 0-938086-99-5

Printed in Japan

Library of Congress Cataloging-in-Publication Data

Andújar, Gloria.
  La Jolla.

  Includes index.
  1. La Jolla (San Diego, Calif.)--Description--Guide-
books. 2. San Diego (Calif.)--Description--Guide-books.
I. Sullivan, Jeremiah, 1954-   . II. Title.
F869.S22A55 1987   979.4'98   86-22207
ISBN 0-938086-99-5

To Julio — who makes all things possible.

Gloria A. Anzaldúa

Preface

The etymology of *La Jolla* (pronounced lah ho-yah) is as colorful as the town itself. There are three interpretations that seem plausible, and defending any one of them can rouse a heated discussion from even the most indifferent resident.

Anthropologists confirm that metates and other stone utensils discovered in this vicinity indicate that there was an Indian settlement, and perhaps even a burial ground, in La Jolla as long as 3,000 years ago. Some propose that *la jolla* was the early Spaniards' rendition of the Indian word for cave—*hoya*. The dramatic caves along La Jolla's shoreline certainly may have inspired the Indians to call their settlement "the place of many caves."

The earliest Spanish settlers of San Diego first referred to the little Indian village in La Jolla as *la ranchería*, which is basically a collection of huts. Indian women would travel into today's Presidio Hill in Old Town with pots stacked high on their heads for use by the garrison that was stationed there. The Spaniards had no buckets, so the ornamented clay pots crafted by the Indians became invaluable for transporting water from the river. Soon the Spaniards dubbed *la ranchería* as *la olla* (the pot)—the place from which the pots came. The junction of the two vowels made pronunciation clumsy, so eventually the spelling evolved into La Jolla.

Yet, others contend that *La Jolla* is a corruption of the Castilian *hoya*, which is a common geographical term that refers to a hollow on the coast worn away by waves. This term, variously spelled, appears repeatedly in several Spanish maps and documents of early California. Mission and land grant records, especially a Poscoe Map dating back to 1870, indicate the location of *La Joya* (Pueblo Lots 1286 and 1288) in a hollow surrounded by hills close to today's Beach and Tennis Club.

The letters ll and y are totally separate entities in today's Spanish alphabet; but they were commonly interchangeable as late as the nineteenth century, which can add credence to the interpretation of your choice.

Although there is no evidence to support it, many locals firmly adhere to the belief that their town is named "the jewel," after the Spanish word *joya*. No matter which interpretation you support, one cannot deny that La Jolla, in one short century, has become justifiably recognized as "the jewel of the Pacific."

Records indicate that La Jolla was actually part of the Pueblo Lands of the City of San Diego and that Samuel Sizer purchased the first lot, approximately eighty acres, in 1869 for a mere one hundred dollars. The lot directly south of Sizer's number 1259, was purchased by his brother Daniel on the same date at the same price of $1.25 an acre.

The first Santa Fe railroad train pulled into San Diego in 1885, and almost immediately word of the area's qualities spread throughout the country. Settlers began arriving in increasing numbers. Tourists soon began riding through tall grass, sagebrush and huge fields of wild flowers to picnic on the beach and explore the cliffs and caves of "La Jolla Park." Although water was scarce and the Santa Fe was not very near, La Jolla offered many natural advantages that were perceptively visualized by an Eastern developer, Frank Terrill Botsford. Scarcely three months after arriving in San Diego, Botsford and his partner George Heald bought most of La Jolla. They surveyed it through the Pacific Coast Land Bureau and prepared it for a now-historic land auction. The first lot was auctioned on April 30, 1887, to a C.A. Wetmore for $1,250, and the boom was on. Soon after, roads were paved and trees lavishly planted. The hundred-room La Jolla Park Hotel was built, a few private residences went up and soon there were cottages to rent. Tourists came to enjoy the new Pacific playground, and La Jolla grew into a community.

The first available population estimate records 1,300 residents and 264 structures in August 1905. During the '20s and '30s, La Jolla developed into a pleasant, quiet village inhabited by colorful characters. The '40s began the modern development of La Jolla as the end of World War II brought thousands of ex-servicemen and their families back to where they had been trained. The veterans' return brought about a real estate boom that transformed La Jolla from a cozy, seaside village of 2,000 residents in the '30s to a more cosmopolitan 11,000 in the '50s. As the University of California campus on the Torrey Pines mesa grew and gained prestige in the '60s, it attracted noted professors and scientists from around the world. The renowned Scripps Clinic and venerable Salk Institute did the same. More recently, dozens of new think-tank industries have added to the immigrating brain trust. The first-class cadre of scientists, humanists and professionals who make La Jolla their home could fill pages of *Who's Who*. Despite the accelerated growth of the last decades, La Jolla insists on remaining small and carefully monitoring growth at all levels through a town plan. The twenty-first century is expected to be greeted by not more than an estimated 32,000 La Jollans.

La Jolla is blessed by nature with unrivaled beauty. Since its earliest days, residents have labored tirelessly to preserve its charm and improve its quality of life. Today, La Jolla ranks as one of the most prestigious communities along the California coast; people nation-wide refer to it with superlative accolades. La Jolla truly is a masterpiece that combines a sophisticated, casual elegance with Old World traditions and an intangible air of good breeding. Although it is difficult to identify any one quality that sets La Jolla apart, it is perhaps the diversity and energy of its residents that make it shine. Whether working for one of the national service clubs, cultural foundations, charitable organizations, medical auxiliaries, churches, schools, or the town council, La Jollans are actively engaged in service and committed to shaping its future. They represent a group of caring, well-educated people whose interests, energy and ideas ultimately affect every facet of community life.

The near-perfect weather, exceptional natural environment and diverse man-made structures of La Jolla attract visitors, making it a mecca of tourist luxury. La Jolla has never lost the friendliness of earlier small-town days. It welcomes visitors year-round who escape blizzard-blown winters or unbearably hot summers. Tourists immediately sense that there is something very special in La Jolla, and newcomers intuitively know that this is where they're meant to be. Once you've visited, return seems imperative.

This book is a photographic tribute to La Jolla — a profile of the assets that are singularly hers. With it the author salutes this remarkable jewel and hopes to instill a sense of continuity and pride among even the youngest La Jollan.

Gloria Andújar

From Above

La Jolla, sitting proudly on the edge of the Pacific Ocean, presents one extraordinary panorama after another. It occupies roughly seven miles of narrow, curving coastline that alternates sandy beaches, steep bluffs, and rocky caves. Located 14 miles northwest of downtown San Diego, 115 miles south of Los Angeles and 30 miles north of Mexico, La Jolla's unofficial boundaries extend from the hills curving inland above Pacific Beach on the south to Del Mar along Torrey Pines Road on the north and from the Pacific Ocean east to just beyond Interstate 5. Its 6,482 acres contain approximately 12,460 housing units, which are shared by 30,000 La Jollans. Less than 700 vacant acres remain.

Weather blesses the region with its near perfection; a comfortable 64° is the mean temperature and the days dawn clear on the average of 265 times a year. There is only a 14° spread between summer highs of 71° and winter lows of 57° The annual ocean temperature is 62° warming up to 68° during the summer months. But even on the warmest days, the entire village is bathed in gentle ocean breezes.

La Jolla's scenery is varied and exquisitely beautiful. This masterpiece of nature combines picturesque canyons with an ever-changing sea, sandy coves with rocky caves and mesas with distant mountains rising into glorious skies. La Jolla's casually sophisticated ambiance and spectacular scenery rival Europe's famed Riviera.

A bird's-eye view of La Jolla as it is today makes it difficult to envision the collection of tiny cottages and dusty chaparral that it was only a hundred years ago.

1

La Valencia Hotel

La Valencia began life during a land boom. Its graceful wrought-iron gates were first opened in 1926 as Los Apartamentos de Sevilla; its grand opening on Christmas Day was a lavish affair. Noted architect William Templeton Johnson, respected for his authentic research in the classic Spanish schools, designed the $200,000 structure for owners MacArthur Gorton and Ray Wiltsie who had gone out on a limb to build it and had provided for everything but the Great Depression. Before losing their pink lady, however, Gorton and Wiltsie managed to acquire and refurbish the adjacent Cabrillo Hotel, which was an original Irving Gill design, and to build a distinctive mosaic tile tower that remains as one of La Jolla's landmarks.

During the war years, La Valencia's lobby was filled with uniformed soldiers on their way to battle, and the cottages nearby were rented to their awaiting wives. The tower served as a spotting post for enemy aircraft and was manned around the clock by hotel staff, guests and townsfolk.

Always a haven for Hollywood's gods and goddesses, La Valencia enjoyed one of its most glamorous eras during the 1950s when it became the social headquarters of stars such as Gregory Peck, Ida Lupino, David Niven, Groucho Marx, Tallulah Bankhead, Mary Pickford, Charles Laughton, Greta Garbo and cadres more.

Its impeccable pink exterior, welcoming and genuine decor, lush flowering patios, individually accoutered guest rooms and the permanence of its staff combine to exude the warmth of an Old World home to which a cult of loyal devotees return year after year. The grand old lady, rich in tradition and charm, continues to host La Jolla's most distinguished visitors. Now with an international roster of guests that includes royalty, La Valencia maintains a full house year-round with notables such as Melvin Laird, Walter Cronkite, Alexander Haig, Dustin Hoffman, Beverly Sills and Robert McNamara.

But La Valencia's gracious elegance is perhaps best savored by local residents for it is La Jolla's village pub, the town meeting place of now third and fourth generation La Jollans. In any of La Valencia's three fine restaurants, dedicated patrons continue to enjoy outstanding cuisine coupled with an attentive staff who know all regulars by name.

High above the blue Pacific Ocean, amid Mediterranean charm, is preserved one of La Jolla's finest traditions—her very own pink lady.

Ellen Browning Scripps Park

With spacious grass and beach areas and the spectacular views it affords, Scripps Park is a favorite of La Jollans, young and old. Its seaside gazebos host the town's most memorable picnics.

In 1904 the park was a place for tents, manure piles, tins and bottles. But largely through the efforts of local resident Walter Lieber, it was cleared and adorned by a row of slender Washington palms. In 1909 La Jollans celebrated Lincoln's 100th birthday by erecting the park's flagstaff; and in 1927, on the occasion of Ellen Browning Scripps's ninety-first birthday, the San Diego Park Commission bestowed her name on the dear little park. On her 100th birthday, the landmark Monterey cypress was planted posthumously honoring her unselfish efforts to improve the quality of life in La Jolla.

Women such as Kate Sessions, Anna Held Heinrich and Eleanore Mills played a vital role in developing La Jolla into the thriving community it is today. None, however, deserve more credit than Ellen Browning Scripps. Described as La Jolla's fairy godmother and resident philanthropist, the remarkable early citizen possessed both wisdom and foresight. Her ways were humble and unassuming, yet her accomplishments are countless. Her name is synonymous with the most respected medical, scientific, academic and cultural institutions. A few of her local benefactions include The Athenaeum, The La Jolla Womens Club, The Children's Pool, Torrey Pines State Park, The Bishop's School, The La Jolla Public Library, Scripps Memorial Hospitals, Scripps Clinic and Research Foundation, The La Jolla Recreation Center, Scripps Institution of Oceanography and large contributions to a myriad of causes and groups. No one can estimate what her advent meant to La Jolla, or exactly how much money Miss Ellen donated to her philanthropies, but it was surely in the millions. La Jolla was truly blessed by the presence of Ellen Browning Scripps, one of those rare human beings whose unselfish commitment leaves an imprint on civilization.

John Cole's Book Shop

Both the bookshop and the historic cottage that houses it are rightfully considered La Jolla treasures. Built in 1903 as one of several cottages on the South Moulton Villa estate of Ellen Browning Scripps, this charming structure housed her guests before becoming her sister Virginia's home. The spirited Miss Virginia had a passion for purple, which inspired her to personally plant the sixty-foot covered walkway with lush, lavender wisteria vines and to christen her home "Wisteria Cottage." In addition to temporarily serving as a rectory, the cozy cottage was home to the remarkable Balmer School for nearly twenty years, which later became the cornerstone of today's La Jolla Country Day School.

Wisteria Cottage, now designated a historic site, has housed John Cole's Book Shop since it moved from Ivanhoe Street in 1966. Its small, irregularly shaped rooms and inviting nooks and crannies are brimming with rare works, international folk art, handsome art books, unusual toys from around the world and the latest best-sellers. Unique cards, wrapping papers, bookmarks, puzzles and seasonal lore fill intriguing antique chests throughout the store. The warm and welcoming children's room overflows with a remarkable collection and beckons youngsters to browse, play or simply daydream while gazing at the sea below.

In the true tradition of La Jolla merchants, three generations of Coles provide quality individualized attention that makes locals feel like old-time friends and visitors feel welcome. In addition to being a treasure trove of local lore, Wisteria Cottage on any given day may host a puppet show on its palm-studded lawn, an autograph party for world-famous author Marguerite Henry or a craft sale under its vine-gnarled entryway. The sixty-year-old wooden hobby horse, which has rocked generations of La Jollans outside its doors, and the diversified collection within are all part of the distinct Cole touch that continues to beckon readers of all ages.

La Jolla
Country Day School

The children of La Jolla first congregated for school at different sites, such as private homes and vacant stores, as early as 1894. La Jolla has come a long way since the days of its first "little red school house" on Herschel Avenue, and now it boasts one of the finest primary and secondary school systems in the nation. Over 92% of the area's graduating seniors go on to college. To accommodate its under-nineteen population of 2,500, La Jolla counts on no less than twelve outstanding public, private and parochial schools.

La Jolla Country Day School ranks among the nation's leading college preparatory independent schools for students in preschool through twelfth grade. Tracing its roots to the Balmer School, which began as a small primary school eventually housed in today's John Cole's Book Shop, Country Day moved to its present location on Genesee Avenue in 1964. In addition to a full-size gymnasium, an 11,000-volume library, an amphitheater and independent buildings for music, art and science, the serene twenty-four-acre campus has its own tennis courts, eight acres of playing fields and one of San Diego's two observatories.

Today, in its sixtieth year, La Jolla Country Day School enrolls over 700 students. Following Louise Balmer's tradition of stimulating intellectual curiosity and fostering a dedication to learning, it prepares youngsters to live and work effectively in an ever-changing world.

Prospect Street

Prospect, one of eight streets whose name has remained unchanged since La Jolla was laid out in 1887, was probably the site of its very first cottages and the railroad depot. Today, within a few minutes walk, are clustered some of the nation's finest specialty shops, restaurants, office complexes and art galleries.

La Jolla came alive as an art colony as early as 1894 when the German fräulein Anna Held Heinrich built her house and named it "The Green Dragon" after one of noted author Beatrice Harraden's stories. Anna, known for her friendliness and hospitality, continued to add houses until she had a large cluster on her hillside above the cove, which offered inspiration and shelter to a colony of famous artists.

Artists still continue their pilgrimages to La Jolla and are represented in more than a dozen distinctive galleries and three museums. Ever-growing exhibitions line both Prospect and Girard of avant garde, traditional, western and contemporary artwork as well as photography, exquisite crafts and ancient arts. Adjacent to the Green Dragon's own majestic eucalyptus, planted and nurtured by Anna Held herself, is The Jones Gallery, which features oil paintings, watercolors and sculptures of nineteenth and twentieth century American realists.

La Jolla Cove

Pockets of sand collect all along La Jolla's rocky coastline, but perhaps most fascinating for its natural beauty is the Cove. Surrounded by magnificent cliffs, the protected Cove is a favorite spot for snorkelers who flipper out only a few dozen yards to grassy reefs and abundant marine life. From above, the Cove also offers prime vantage points from which to view the annual whale migration.

The Cove became popular as early as 1899 when the railway built the first flight of wooden stairs down Devil's Slide, and the bounty of exquisite abalone below made the precipitous climb worthwhile. The Cove started to draw national attention in 1916 when it first served as the site of the Roughwater Swim. Now considered the largest open swimming event in the country, this challenging race attracts some 1,500 contestants each summer plus hundreds of admiring spectators. Veteran swimmers claim that the one-mile triangular course offers a unique setting for roughwater maneuvering in an unprotected current.

La Jolla
Recreation Center

Ellen Browning Scripps wanted to make the children happy by providing them a place that they could look upon as their own, where they could romp and play in the fresh air. And so the La Jolla Playground, as it was then known, was one of her early benefactions, first opening to the public in the summer of 1915.

Designed in a modified California mission style by Irving and Louis Gill, the building holds significant value to architectural historians. The playground itself is claimed as the first public playground of its kind and a model for many others.

Since its Fourth of July grand opening celebration seventy-two years ago, the grounds have been used continuously by young and old alike. Here, La Jollans have enjoyed weekly dances, festivals, parades, contests and traditional Christmas celebrations. The center's tennis courts, still in continuous use by racket wielders, were the first site of the La Jolla Tennis Championships. Today, sports, year-round spontaneous activities, classes and all sorts of games are available to La Jollans of all ages just as its benevolent benefactress envisioned.

Because she steadfastly refused to accept public testimonials, it was difficult for people to show Miss Scripps their appreciation for her many philanthropies. A simple bronze fountain of a child scooping water for the birds to drink was sculpted by James Porter and dedicated in tribute to Ellen Browning Scripps in 1926. Every school child in La Jolla was asked to contribute a penny toward this tasteful memorial.

Scripps Clinic and Research Foundation

Scripps Clinic and Research Foundation is among the oldest and largest private research institutions in the United States. Remarkable research laboratories, a major hospital and a sophisticated outpatient facility are housed within a single, modern, five-acre complex on the Torrey Pines mesa.

Displaying her characteristic foresight, philanthropist Ellen Browning Scripps predicted that the emerging science of biochemistry was destined to transform the entire field of medicine. With her impetus and funds, a small, single-story facility on Prospect Street opened its doors in 1924. Known as the Scripps Metabolic Clinic, and staffed by seven professionals, the modest facility offered special diagnostic services and conducted some research, primarily in diabetes.

In its sixty-three-year history, the single-specialty Clinic has become an internationally renown health care and biochemical research institution with more than 3,000 employees in twelve locations throughout San Diego County, with expertise spanning over fifty fields of medicine and surgery. In an effort to maintain high standards of excellence, Scripps Clinic attracts thousands of clinicians and scientists from all corners of the world who participate each year in more than 1,250 seminars and symposiums.

La Jolla is proud to boast some of the world's most important science and research facilities, which from often humble beginnings have successfully emerged to preserve the quality of life and have ultimately improved the human condition.

Torrey Pines State Park

Clinging tenaciously to the rocky soil on the cliffs and canyons overlooking the Pacific is La Jolla's oldest resident, the torrey pine. This rarest of conifers grows naturally in only one other place in the world, on Santa Rosa Island 30 miles southwest of Santa Barbara, in two small relic forests.

After careful study of the unique trees, physician and botanist Charles Parry successfully identified them in 1850 and named them "pinus torrey-ana," in honor of John Torrey of New York's Columbia University, one of the country's leading botanists. As early as 1899 the city of San Diego declared its interest in protecting the rare pine and set aside the 369 acres upon which they were growing as a public park. In the 1920s Ellen Browning Scripps embraced a movement to further preserve this valuable natural heritage extending along the cliffs north of the city between La Jolla and Del Mar. Today nearly 1,000 acres of canyons, mesas and scenic trails and over three miles of sandy beach provide refuge for local wildlife and outdoor enthusiasts.

Recognizable for its long, stout grayish-green needles that grow five in a cluster, the majestic torrey pine is a rare remnant of past ages that mysteriously chose La Jolla to plant its rugged roots. Their singular beauty, might and grace may be but another simple gift from He who smiled so benevolently on La Jolla.

Central University Library

The University of California, San Diego is one of the major teaching and research institutions in the United States. It is internationally recognized for work in the physical, biological and social sciences; the humanities and the arts; engineering; medicine and oceanography.

Although the university traces its roots to a team of Berkeley zoologists who set up a summer marine station in 1903 (which became Scripps Institution of Oceanography), it was not until 1964 that the first 181 undergraduates began their studies in three newly completed high-rise buildings and in barracks and Quonset huts left behind by the Navy. Today, more than 2,000 eminent scholars, including five Nobel laureates, teach over 14,000 students in specialized programs and departments. UCSD's main campus now extends over 1,936 verdant acres in northern La Jolla. Its links and contributions to the community are significant. UCSD provides local industry with highly trained personnel and the opportunity to update the skills of current employees. Its calendar flows with artistic and cultural events, and the campus serves as a rich educational and informational resource for the community at large.

Hovering for all the world like an intelligence-stocked spaceship from another planet is the Central University Library, which was designed by William L. Pereira Associates to convey the idea that powerful hands are holding aloft knowledge itself. Featured in Time magazine for its unique design, the impressive structure is the flagship of a fleet of UCSD research libraries that house approximately 1,700,000 volumes and serve more than two and a half million students, faculty and community members.

Mary, Star of the Sea

The parish compound of Mary, Star of the Sea, which is unique for its architectural and decorative excellence, occupies the northwest corner of Kline and Girard.

Designed by Carleton Monroe Winslow in a spirit reminiscent of early California missions, the existing church was completed in late 1937 and dedicated by San Diego's first bishop, Charles Francis Buddy. The mosaic mural over the church's main entrance is of special attraction to passersby. This original fresco by the great Mexican muralist Alfredo Ramos Martínez depicts the Virgin Mary standing erect in prayer, flanked by two attendant angels against a vivid blue sky and stylized Pacific waves. A shining star and the brown hills of the California coastline complete this remarkable work of art. However, twenty-five years of salt air and radiant sun caused irreparable fading of the original pigments. An exact replica in mosaic tiles was created in Rome from intricate measurements and large-scale color photographs and painstakingly installed in 1962.

The dominant element in the church's interior decor is a magnificent, neo-Byzantine mural executed by the renown ecclesiastical artist John Henry de Rosen, who also decorated the Pope's private chapel at Castel Gandolfo. Sparkling with gold and silver leaf and glowing with reds and blues, this symbolic work seems to compliment the almost austere simplicity of the church itself. The magnificent red mantle embroidered with silver roses is clasped at Our Lady's breast and boasts an actual jeweled silver brooch with a sapphire in the center representing the mariner's star. This Stella Polaris is a work of art that was designed, created and donated by a noted La Jolla jeweler.

Of historical interest is the solid brass bell atop the "Aula" building adjoining the main church, which was brought from Spain by the early Franciscan padres and bears the inscription "Jesus • 1690 • Maria."

Mary, Star of the Sea and All Hallows are La Jolla's two Roman Catholic parishes. Both provide quality Kindergarten through eighth grade academies in the parochial tradition.

Torrey Pines Glider Port

Undoubtedly, La Jolla's first glider was the daring Frazier Curtis who in 1910 attached a pair of wings with a harness to his shoulders and flew short distances from the slopes of Mt. Soledad.

A park area over the sandstone bluffs north of La Jolla, between Torrey Pines Park and La Jolla Farms, is designated specifically for today's gliders. The air currents are made possible by strong updrafts of prevailing westerly winds that meet the 360-foot coastal cliffs, creating ideal conditions for piloting. The graceful navigators riding the sea breezes in their brightly colored gliders attract admiring spectators up and down the Torrey Pines shoreline year-round.

If you dream of soaring like a bird free of the earth without powered assistance, you can register for flight lessons and brace yourself for the adventure of a lifetime. Those qualified, but less daredevilish, can enjoy the famous soaring site for launching radio-controlled model sailplanes.

La Jolla Library

The La Jolla Library is the oldest, and perhaps most valued, public institution in town. In 1898 benefactress Florence Sawyer donated a sixty-by-sixty-foot lot on the corner of Wall and Girard, a collection of books and a small, furnished wooden building called The Reading Room. With almost everyone in town present, La Jolla's first library opened its doors in July 1899. But the enthusiastic community soon outgrew the charming little structure, and in 1921 William Templeton Johnson designed the existing building. Bibliophile Ellen Browning Scripps donated the two adjoining lots that make up the present site and substantially endowed the building fund together with matching community contributions.

Housing an extensive collection of classics, recreational reading, reference materials on almost every subject, periodicals and recordings, the library has been a place for all La Jollans to learn and grow. Generations have enjoyed story hours, fascinating children's programs, lectures, seminars and a variety of cultural events.

In 1988 La Jolla will proudly dedicate the 10,000-square-foot Florence Riford Library on Draper Avenue, which will reflect a traditional style of light-colored stucco walls and a red tile roof. Continuing its eighty-nine-year tradition, the third La Jolla Library will serve future generations as a vital cultural and educational center.

The Children's Pool

Prominent among the splendid facilities donated to La Jollans by Ellen Browning Scripps is a safe, shallow wading pool on an ample, crescent-shaped beach. While waves pound the cliffs and caves, bathers can swim and play in this quiet cove just around the point. A favorite haven for families with toddlers, the pool is protected by the Pacific surf and winds by a reinforced concrete breakwater that curves seaward for 300 feet from a bluff at the edge of the ocean to a natural low barrier reef. Access to the pool is provided by a reinforced stairway from the top of the bluff down to the sandy beach.

In 1923 Ellen Browning Scripps commissioned a report from engineer Hiram Newton Savage on the feasibility, practicability and estimated cost of a bathing pool in La Jolla. His report contained details on a number of the world's most important breakwaters and summarized his studies of these structures. From these surveys, detailed plans and sectional drawings were prepared. The location of the structure was carefully considered relative to its purpose, foundation conditions, topography and economy of design. Invitations to bid were sent to contractors experienced in marine work, and the job was eventually awarded to W.M. Ledbetter & Company of Los Angeles. At a total cost of $67,000, the pool was dedicated to the advancement of the health and happiness of La Jolla's children in June 1931. Since then it has been enjoyed daily by children of residents and visitors alike. The railed walkway along the top of the breakwater is an ideal spot to hear and feel the mist of the roaring waves as they hit the jetty.

Casa de Mañana

Since its beginning in 1924, this luxurious, graceful seaside resort became popular throughout the country for its homelike atmosphere, outstanding cuisine and remarkable charm. Designed by Edgar Ullrich, the rambling Spanish colonial buildings set along the coast were the dream of Isabel Morrison, who furnished her castle with ornate Spanish and Italian furniture from Hollywood movie sets. Perhaps it was this touch of home that attracted stage stars and celebrities such as Mary Astor, Ginger Rogers, and Rita Hayworth. With its flowing fountains, elegant archways, flowering courtyards and elaborate cottages, the Casa remained the scene of local social activities until World War II when it housed an officer's clubroom and civil defense classes.

In 1953 the distinctive hotel was extensively remodeled, reopening as one of the world's most beautiful retirement homes. In one main building plus seven other residential structures, the oceanfront complex now offers hotel-type accommodations, communal activities and health services for over 200 residents.

La Jolla Boulevard

Known in the early days as Olive Avenue and later renamed after the civil engineer Simeon Borden, today's La Jolla Boulevard is one of the two arterials serving the central village. The Bird Rock business district, which derived its name from an offshore formation that has long been a favored nesting place for seabirds, serves the needs of a large residential area in southern La Jolla.

Often referred to by locals as "restaurant row," the boulevard's three-block stretch between Camino de la Costa and Midway boasts no less than nineteen restaurants including some of La Jolla's finer dining spots. From sushi to burritos or tortellini to escargots, gourmands can select from an outstanding variety of cuisines and prices. Certainly, restaurants contribute substantially to La Jolla's economy and to its quality of life. Competing with the finest food capitals of the world, La Jolla abounds with exquisite restaurants and casual eateries.

The southernmost stretch of La Jolla Boulevard, adjoining the community of Pacific Beach, is home to several convenient motels which are in walking distance to Bird Rock's renown beaches.

United Methodist Church

This may very well be the only church in the world that holds the unique distinction of having once been both a railroad depot and a restaurant bar. In 1953 seven devoted Methodists convened in one of the lounges at the Casa de Mañana and envisioned a fellowship that would reach out in service to the community, nation and world. With great energy, and at a great personal sacrifice, the small congregation raised sufficient funds to purchase the San Carlos substation on La Jolla Boulevard that was a waiting room for the trolley line of the old San Diego Electric Railway. Originally designed by architect Eugene Hoffman, the charming terminal building was temporarily converted into the church's first sanctuary.

In the following years, the growing congregation bought the adjacent La Plaza Restaurant and El Toro Bar. Housed in an L-shaped, Spanish style building and featuring meats charred over an open grill, La Plaza was once a favored haven of writers, authors and celebrities such as Billy Wilder, Max Miller, Raymond Chandler, Jonathan Latimer and J. Edgar Hoover. In 1959 enterprising church members rolled up their sleeves to remodel these charming old Plaza structures into a sanctuary and library with the old station becoming a chapel.

Since then, the United Methodist Church has enlarged considerably and added a Christian Education building that houses an innovative program for children ages two through five. The present sanctuary, offices and Memorial Hall were completed in 1970, and the Plaza building became Fellowship Hall. By using mission-style roofing and stucco walls, compatibility was maintained with the Spanish heritage visible in the earlier buildings. Particularly attractive are the olive-gnarled courts that foster the warm tradition of lingering in fellowship before and after services.

In keeping with the vision of its pioneer leaders, the now 500-strong congregation has become increasingly involved in both local and international outreach programs that minister to the spiritual and physical needs of various groups.

Boating

Ocean-related recreation and sports are major elements of the La Jolla life-style. Off-shore waters provide exceptional fishing year-round, and the sheltering promontory of Alligator Head at the Cove permits small boat launching for anglers in quest of albacore, marlin or tuna.

Many La Jollans are ardent yachtsmen with great enthusiasm for sailing anything from skiffs to ocean racers, which has resulted in several excellent records in international events.

On most any weekend, the natural beauty of La Jolla's dramatic coast is enjoyed by pleasure boaters. There is no better spot for capturing La Jolla's magnificent twilight and sunset than from a floating craft on the seemingly infinite Pacific.

The Athenaeum

Tucked in from Wall Street, directly next to the library, is one of La Jolla's cultural treasures. Architect William Lumpkins designed the delightfully charming Athenaeum in 1957 at the request of the Library Association to house a nucleus of rare books and manuscripts in music and art.

Today's Athenaeum boasts one of the finest collections on the West Coast of art and music books, classical and popular recordings, compact discs, muscial scores, foreign and domestic periodicals, opera libretti, photographs, old song sheets and video tapes. Both members and visitors enjoy browsing through the complete works of Bach in German, researching with the latest specialized dictionaries or listening to their favorite sonata.

In addition to constantly improving its carefully cataloged collection, the Athenaeum provides the community with a variety of enriching programs, including art exhibits, demonstrations, concerts, lectures, book sales, gallery tours and outstanding children's events.

The Athenaeum is a charming refuge that refreshes the soul and stimulates the creative imagination. It endeavors to leave La Jollans a legacy that will nurture and encourage the artistic spirit.

The Salk Institute

Just north of the UCSD campus, atop a majestic canyon overlooking the Pacific, rises one of La Jolla's strongest architectural statements, The Salk Institute. It was designed by Louis Kahn in 1960 to create a unique environment that would stimulate original thinking.

With a staff of nearly 500, which includes Nobel laureates and many internationally recognized scientific leaders, The Salk Institute is one of the world's outstanding facilities for biological research. Results that have emerged from the institute's nineteen research laboratories have contributed significantly to the solution of health problems in areas such as cancer, stress, growth deficiencies, virus infections and genetic defects. Since The Salk Institute maintains close scientific ties with other research institutions worldwide, it attracts visiting scientists who add a constant source of new ideas, keeping it at the cutting edge of research technology.

Within its rich intellectual environment and modern laboratory facilities, The Salk Institute provides a unique climate for fostering scientific innovation that ultimately improves the quality of life for us all.

Torrey Pines Golf Course

La Jolla's benign year-round climate and spectacular natural setting make it a sportsman's paradise. Since its earliest days, La Jolla has been a spawning ground for athletes of virtually every sport some of whom have achieved accomplishments of national acclaim.

Records indicate that early La Jollans were putting the green as far back as 1899 on a course running along Prospect. Today, they boast two, including an eighteen-hole championship course on the cliffs overlooking the ocean that has been ranked among the best public courses in the country and the equal of Carmel's famed Pebble Beach. Torrey Pines is host to the annual Andy Williams Open, which dates back to 1952 and has attracted such world champions as Arnold Palmer, Jack Nicklaus, Tom Watson and Johnny Miller. The exacting four-day Open, with its half million dollar total purse, attracts not only the world's top golfers, but thousands of enthusiastic spectators and hundreds of members of the international press. The prestigious sporting event is nationally telecast bringing La Jolla and its mild February weather to everyone's attention.

Many giants of the game have been born and nurtured here, often teeing off as toddlers with their dads at the picturesque La Jolla Country Club course.

La Jolla Presbyterian

Both spiritually and architecturally inspiring, La Jolla churches represent over fifteen major denominations. In 1889 the seaside resort wasn't sufficiently populated to justify formal church organization, and a preaching station at a vacant store was shared by roving ministers.

It was not until 1905 that ten devoted Presbyterians incorporated their first church — initially a wood-floored tent. It wasn't long before they moved into a small, open-raftered, three-room frame building on Girard and Torrey Pines, which came to be known as the Little Brown Church. After numerous moves around the village, the old church finally settled at the existing Draper Avenue site where it was replaced in 1928 by the present structure.

Since then, property and buildings have been added to accommodate the energetic congregation, which now numbers approximately 4000. In Christian togetherness, youths, singles, families and seniors are committed to a wide range of fellowship programs both at home and around the world.

Avenida de la Playa

From the Muirlands to Hermosa and from the Farms to the Shores, La Jollans live in a variety of residential areas that extend over its 6,482 acres. Although best known for its superior beach and the famous red-roofed Beach and Tennis Club, La Jolla Shores is a neighborhood that seems almost a community unto itself. It originally consisted of only a few homes scattered on the flatland behind the beach, but it has filled in solidly with homes spreading up the slope along both sides of La Jolla Shores Drive.

Within approximately five acres along both sides of Avenida de la Playa is a charming neighborhood business area of specialty shops and professional offices. The small lots, low roof lines, colorful plantings and varied building styles that display wood and other natural materials all contribute to the unique and pleasing character of the Shores. Although planned as a small neighborhood facility to accommodate the needs of area residents, the center of the Shores now houses one of southern California's finest restaurants and thus welcomes an extended community of visitors.

La Jolla Shores

Perhaps the most popular spot along La Jolla's coast is its flattest and safest swimming beach, attracting thousands of people on any given summer Sunday.

Old citizens of La Jolla report that Long Beach, as the Shores was originally known, was considered by the Chinese as an ideal spot for smuggling opium in the shadows of dusk. But today it is divers, joggers, fishermen and tai chi students that take full advantage of the Shores early morning calm. Volleyball enthusiasts organize games and tournaments, playing from dawn until dusk on this favored stretch.

In 1951 a large tract of land bordering the sea was donated by Florence Scripps Kellogg in memory of her husband, and since then, Kellogg Park has been the site of family picnics, kite flying, games and other leisure activities.

Whether gathering shells, leisurely strolling along the water's rippling edge or building the sandcastle of one's dreams, La Jolla Shores combines all the best qualities of sand and sea.

Casa de las Joyas

It is said that the architectural feature that most readily draws the eye is the dome. The thousands who daily pass by it would agree that the three-domed "House of Jewels," now a familiar landmark off Torrey Pines, is an attention-getter indeed. Visitors are always surprised to learn that the sparkling white edifice is a comfortable private home and not an exotic Moslem temple or an *Arabian Nights* palace.

Herbert Palmer, an enigmatic British-born architect, designed some of La Jolla's finest Mediterranean-style homes as well as the popular Arcade building, which runs from Girard to Prospect. Inspired by his fervent memory of the Taj Mahal, which he once idolized while in India, Palmer designed and almost single-handedly built his dream house in 1927 on a magnificent La Jolla Shores hillside. He paved its floors with thousands of exquisite pebbles and shells carried up from the beach and chiseled its walls with his favorite philosophies. Its circular walls, intricately carved panels, enchanting court-yards and mushrooming domes combine to project the elusive ideal sought by Palmer.

The mysterious "Casa de las Joyas," as it was christened by its master, has inspired many tall tales in its sixty-year history. Some old-timers affirm that a king's ransom is buried within its foundation walls, while others recall its days as a bootlegger's hideaway during Pro-hibition and a celebrated gambling casino. Amusing rumors and speculation about this House of Many Legends still arise, but it is indisputable that the genial Palmer injected a touch of the exotic Far East into a setting more commonly known for its ranch-style and contemporary designs. The majestic retreat on La Jolla's busiest thoroughfare perhaps is a life's monument to its creator, who firmly believed that we must all "do something to show that we have lived."

Scripps Institution of Oceanography

Located on 170 acres of prime, oceanfront land just below UCSD's main campus is the nation's oldest and largest institution devoted to oceanography, the world's foremost center for marine sciences.

Founded in 1903 through the efforts of Berkeley biology professor William Ritter and a group of prominent San Diegans, the then independent biological research laboratory became an integral part of the University of California in 1912 when it received its present name in recognition of the support of Ellen Scripps and her brother Edward.

Over the decades, Scripps research scientists have sailed nearly four million nautical miles throughout the world's oceans, observing environments and their inhabitants and retrieving specimens and collecting data. Today over 1,000 staff members occupy sixty-five buildings where researchers from many nations conduct studies. The Scripps Library ranks among the country's leading marine science libraries.

Especially popular among generations of La Jollans is the institution's unique aquarium, which draws more than 300,000 visitors a year. Coastal underwater habitats are recreated in breathtaking exhibits. In addition to an onshore man-made tide pool, twenty-two marine life tanks, displays that explain advancements in oceanography and a well-stocked bookstore, the Scripps aquarium offers educational tours for school groups and a variety of fascinating summer classes for budding oceanographers. Always attracting prominent visitors, such as Japan's Emperor Hirohito and England's Queen Elizabeth, Scripps Institution of Oceanography is a La Jolla institution that has become a genuine world force in the affairs of man and his environment.

Girard Avenue

La Jolla's first general merchandise store opened its doors in 1894 in a tiny gabled-roof building with a false front. The once one-store town, visited weekly by a number of traveling wagons that supplied meat and produce to its residents, has mushroomed with rows of distinctive shops.

Originally known as Grand, the broad avenue in the downtown business district was renamed in 1900 after American naturalist and zoologist Frederic Girard. Girard, La Jolla's main commercial artery, is lined with rows of relatively small specialty establishments that boast both friendly atmosphere and personalized service. While socializing with the town's oldest merchants, shoppers can pick up goods to supply every conceivable need—a spool of thread, a fresh orchid, the latest best-seller or a five-carat diamond.

More recently, international merchants with large establishments elsewhere have opened stores along Girard in the style of La Jolla's small-town mercantile tradition. Also noteworthy along this three-block stretch are the village's one and only movie theater, the Cove, and its two legendary coffee shops, Harry's and John's.

La Jolla Playhouse
Mandell Weiss Center

The new Mandell Weiss Center for the Performing Arts brings campus and community together, housing both the UCSD Department of Theater and the nationally acclaimed La Jolla Playhouse.

The theater is an art form that has consistently interested La Jollans. Native son Gregory Peck, Dorothy McGuire and Mel Ferrer envisioned an ambitious summer theater which opened in 1947 with an outstanding production of *Night Must Fall* starring Dame May Whitty. Since its initial season, audiences filled the hard wooden seats of the La Jolla High auditorium for first-class plays produced, directed and acted by famous personalities. James Mason, Joseph Cotten, Celeste Holm, David Niven and Olivia de Haviland are but a few of the stars who appeared week after week and drew national attention to La Jolla. The Playhouse flourished as one of the leading summer theaters in America until it temporarily suspended operations in the sixties while plans for building a world-class theater emerged.

Through the vision, vitality an benevolence of community leaders, groups and the university, the 500-seat Mandell Weiss Center opened its doors in 1982 with the most advanced technical facilities available. In its new home, the La Jolla Playhouse has already garnered over sixty awards of excellence, including seven coveted Tony Awards for its extraordinary Broadway production of *Big River: The Adventures of Huckleberry Finn*. It offers La Jollans theatrical excellence few American cities can match.

La Jolla Post Office

La Jolla's first post office was established in 1894 and moved to various locations until its present white stucco building on Wall Street was erected in 1935.

First Postmaster Charles Ritchie would surely be astonished to discover that now over 1,300,000 pieces of mail are handled each week by 125 local employees. Either mounted or on foot, today's carriers make over 20,000 daily deliveries throughout the town's fifty-two routes. La Jolla, although officially a part of San Diego, retains separate post office status with its own individual zip code.

The charming shell-and-seahorse bronze bench outside the post office is perhaps the best spot in town for people watching and enjoying the fragrant eucalyptus. Now prevalent throughout San Diego, these graceful evergreens were imported from Australia in the nineteenth century to provide wood for railroad ties. The scarcity of water made cultivation difficult and many died, but the survivors eventually adapted to the climate and developed into lofty trees. First-time visitors and olfactory-sensitive locals never cease to enjoy the distinctively fresh scent of Wall Street.

La Jolla Underwater Park

Scuba and skin diving are very popular local activities that are promoted by and best enjoyed at the La Jolla Underwater Park. The semitropical waters teem with splendidly colored fish, and spectacular undersea formations provide the diver with a vast spectrum of scenery.

Encompassing approximately 514 acres northward from Goldfish Point to the southern boundary of UCSD's property, the park was dedicated in 1971 by the California Department of Fish and Game with the cooperation of the City of San Diego and is defined by buoys and shore markers.

This look-but-don't-touch ecological area offers undersea life the opportunity to be reestablished and preserves the natural beauty of the coastal area of La Jolla Canyon. In the reserve, the public is prohibited from removing any marine life, geological formation or archeological artifact. Perhaps this visiting school of young bait fish knows that no angler's net ever dips around here. La Jolla's underwater treasures of native flora and fauna are explored and respected by thousands of enthusiastic divers each year.

The Bishop's School

One of La Jolla's most prominent landmarks is The Bishop's School, an 11-acre campus that contains an artistic blend of historic structures and contemporary architecture surrounding a central grass quadrangle.

Made possible by gifts of land and money from philanthropists Ellen and Virginia Scripps, Bishop's was founded in 1909 by the visionary Rt. Rev. Joseph J. Johnson, who strove to create an atmosphere where students were influenced by "simple and beautiful surroundings in a setting of natural loveliness." In the succeeding seventy-seven years, Bishop's founding ideals have held true with education for boys and girls in the seventh through twelfth grades emersed in a rich academic curriculum in the Christian tradition.

World-renown architects Irving Gill and Carleton Winslow designed most of Bishop's buildings employing a modified mission architecture that highlights the simple elegance of arches, a hallmark of Gill's style. Three Bishop's buildings have been designated by the U.S. Department of Interior Historic American Buildings Survey to recognize the merit of Gill's architectural contributions.

The simplicity and proportion of this spectacular campus is enhanced by a luxurious landscape of botanical treasures. Abundantly rich in character and heritage, Bishop's has held on to its valuable traditions and commitment to excellence while graduating generations of students.

Finance

The history of banking in La Jolla dates back to 1907 when the Southern Trust and Savings Bank first offered services to the village's 1,500 residents. Today, there are no fewer than seventeen banks, ten savings and loan associations, and nine members of the New York Stock Exchange with tapes and computerized offices, plus dozens of other stockbrokers and investment counselors.

One of the first steel-and-glass modernistic complexes in town, 1205 Prospect, was completed in 1973 to house several financial institutions including what has now grown into the second largest locally owned independent bank in San Diego, La Jolla Bank & Trust. It received its charter and commenced business in 1973 under a founding board of directors comprised of local entrepreneurs. Today, many milestones and awards later, it offers full services at eleven offices with assets exceeding $300 million. But rapid growth and record profits seem the norm in La Jolla.

At the town's first land sales in 1869, acres were sold for $1.25 apiece. Since then La Jolla has developed into one of the most prestigious and highest priced housing markets in the country. The average residential real estate transaction is currently $400,000. It's no wonder that nearly 750 agents serve La Jolla in 115 local offices. Nearly 1,500 businesses are licensed in La Jolla, and 40% of the households report annual income in excess of $50,000.

In years to come, La Jolla is expected to become one of the nation's leading centers of research and development, attracting headquarters of scientific industries, biomedical health care firms, and diverse high technology companies in addition to many financial and legal firms.

Windandsea Beach

It could be argued that beaches have made La Jolla the tourist mecca that it is. Thousands swarm each year to swim in warm ocean waters and bask in the summer sun. Perhaps it is at Windandsea where the greatest number of local sun worshippers and surfers congregate year-round to enjoy the pleasures of coastal life. During low tides, secret carpets of snowy sand are exposed for sunbathers.

For generations of daring La Jollans, Windandsea has tested their skill and endurance against the challenge of waves. Tossed high by an undersea reef, the consistency of waves made suitable for surfing have made Windandsea the big league of local board riders. Made strong by body surfing and paddling from an early age, tireless young athletes of the Windandsea Surf Team continue to compete successfully at national and world-class levels. Windandsea is home and training ground for these world champions who hold unparalleled records.

But riptides and unpredictable currents at Windandsea often prove too challenging for many young or inexperienced swimmers. As an alternative, beachgoers can wait for low tide when the wonders of marine life are trapped in Windandsea's southernmost tide pools to observe starfish, urchins, hermit crabs, tiny fish, sea hares and countless other fauna.

In addition, Windandsea has been immortalized as the scene of legendary teen parties, several Hollywood movies, novels and songs.

La Jolla Museum of Contemporary Art

Built in 1915 as the South Moulton Villa of Ellen Browning Scripps, this fine example of architect Irving Gill's pioneering modern designs is set in elaborately landscaped grounds framing breathtaking views of the Pacific Ocean.

Village artists and supporters devotedly organized a fund-raising campaign that led to the acquisition of Miss Ellen's property and the foundation of La Jolla's first art center. Initially intended for the benefit of local artists, the small society has evolved since 1941 into a major, internationally recognized arts institution.

The museum's permanent collection focuses on minimal, California, pop and other contemporary developments in art. It includes paintings, drawings, sculptures, photographs and a design collection that focuses on the evolution of the modern chair. In addition to its permanent collection, the museum originates numerous exhibitions and hosts major traveling shows. Over 100,000 visitors a year enjoy not only the museum's fine offerings, education programs and extensive reference library, but also its spectacular site on Prospect Street. The adjacent 500-seat Sherwood Auditorium is host to weekly film series, live performances, chamber music concerts and lectures.

69

Scripps
Memorial Hospitals

Foresighted philanthropist Ellen Browning Scripps opened the doors of a forty-four-bed hospital on Prospect Street in 1924 with the dream of going beyond the activities traditionally expected of a community hospital. Today, from its central forty-acre facility on the Torrey Pines mesa, Scripps Memorial Hospitals encompasses a comprehensive health-care system that reaches throughout San Diego County.

With state-of-the-art techniques and quality research, Scripps provides the community with a continuum of care including preventive medicine and wellness programs, specialized diagnostic and treatment centers, rehabilitation programs, home health care and convalescent facilities. Furthermore, Scripps Memorial Hospitals has been nationally recognized for its community outreach programs, public information lectures, professional symposia and research. With more than twenty specialized facilities, services and programs, Scripps Memorial Hospitals provide the community with health care services committed to preserving our well-being.

With Scripps Hospitals, Scripps Clinic, the Veterans Administration Hospital, the UCSD Medical Center, and numerous private practices, La Jolla boasts an unusual proliferation of medical professionals that represent every specialty.

St. James-by-the-Sea

Now the largest Episcopal church in the San Diego diocese, St. James-by-the-Sea dates back to 1907 when its cornerstone was dedicated on the present triangular lot that was donated by Ellen Browning Scripps. Between 1889 and 1907, however, La Jollans shared the small clapboard Union Church on Girard where services for various denominations were celebrated on alternate Sundays. Virginia Scripps's Wisteria Cottage also temporarily housed the Episcopal congregation until it moved into its first permanent building in 1907.

Designed by Irving Gill, and of outstanding Spanish architecture, today's church houses two sets of remarkable stained glass windows and the Parsons Memorial organ, a custom-built instrument of sixty ranks. The graceful tower, designed from photographs by Louis Gill, is a replica of one destroyed by Porfirio Díaz's forces at Campo Florida, Mexico. Donated by Ellen Browning Scripps as a memorial to her sister Virginia, it houses a historic set of tubular Deagan chimes that are playable from the organ console and from a programmable digital computer.

Through the years, the growing parish has expanded into a variety of supplementary buildings and its tireless works have become well known throughout.

Coast Boulevard

Coast Boulevard extends along the shoreline and provides one of La Jolla's most scenic promenades. Dotted with natural points of interest such as the Cove, Scripps Park and the Children's Pool, Coast Boulevard attracts strollers, joggers, sunset worshippers and even daredevil climbers who spider the rough face of People's Wall. Serious collectors also vow that the crannies between the rocks where Coast Boulevard meets the sea is one of the choicest spots for finding small shells and sea glass.

Coast Boulevard begins at the Cave and Shell Shop from where 133 steps lead down a man-made tunnel to the main chamber of Sunny Jim Cave and the bluff overlooking La Jolla Bay. Its incomparable views and convenient access to both beach and village made Coast Boulevard the site of many "La Jolla originals." Two red cottages facing the Cove, built in 1894 and affectionately known as Red Rest and Red Roost, represent the few remaining architectural treasures that still stand. In contrast, the monumental "939" is a seventeen-story symbol of the struggle between old and new, which resulted in a fifty-foot height limitation on all new construction.

Private Homes

Above all, La Jolla is a place where people live. Its 12,000 homes represent a wide spectrum of architectural endeavors that are as diverse as their occupants. La Jolla is San Diego's most prestigious address, and world-renown master builders have designed many of its homes. William Templeton Johnson, Russell Forester, Irving Gill, Tom Shepherd, Edgar Ullrich and Paul Thoryk are only a few of the greats who have left their mark on La Jolla's distinctive residential areas with a potpourri of styles ranging from Spanish colonial to California ranch to wood-glass contemporary.

Old Hermosa, rich in understated luxury and magnificently groomed landscapes, is home to this ocean-front estate with an enclosed garden-patio shaped in a quadrangle. This comfortable sanctuary, which blends tastefully into the surrounding landscape, came from the same drawing board as La Jolla's "Taj" (see page 50). Herbert Palmer designed both of these exceptional edifices as well as some charming Mediterranean-style homes in the Barber Tract.

Whether built in the 1890s or the 1980s, La Jolla homes reflect the pride and care of their owners. Even the smallest cottage features a beautifully kept patio or blooming garden with flowering trees. Bougainvillea vines, hibiscus bushes and jacaranda trees abound, as do roses, geraniums, lilies, orchids, poppies and ranunculus. It seems that everything flourishes lushly. With spas, swimming pools and often tennis courts, La Jolla's homes are ideally suited for welcoming "amigos," casual entertaining and gracious living.

Mt. Soledad Memorial Cross

Crowning La Jolla's highest point in solemn majesty is a lasting memorial to the dead of both World Wars and the Korean War.

A cross of California redwood was first placed on Mt. Soledad in 1913 where it stood for ten years before it was destroyed by vandals. A sturdier, stucco-over-wood frame cross replaced it but was blown down by blustery winds in 1952. With their characteristic energy, however, La Jollans organized sufficient fund raising and volunteer labor to facilitate erection of a more permanent structure.

Designed in recessed concrete by architect Donald Campbell, the existing cross has a twelve-foot arm spread and stands forty-three feet tall. It was dedicated at the annual Easter Sunday sunrise service of 1954. Rising 822 feet above sea level, the scenic summit affords a spectacular panorama. The cross itself, always illuminated by night, serves as a guiding landmark for residents and visitors alike.

La Jolla Beach and Tennis Club

Tennis, golf and swimming are perhaps the sports in which La Jollans participate the most. Private clubs, such as the La Jolla Beach and Tennis Club and the La Jolla Country Club, provide excellent instruction and facilities for participation in these sports.

Although its first cornerstone was laid in 1927, it was not until 1935 that the foresighted newspaper magnate Frederick William Kellogg purchased and began to develop La Jolla's Beach and Tennis Club. Today, on twenty luxuriously landscaped acres along La Jolla Shores, its members enjoy a nine-hole pitch-and-put course; an outdoor, heated, freshwater championship pool; twelve of the nation's finest tennis courts, the best white-sand beach along the coast, dining and dancing in beautiful, palm-fringed patios, superbly appointed apartments and many other facilities. The La Jolla Beach and Tennis Club is ranked among the finest private clubs in the United States. In addition, it has made La Jolla one of the tennis capitals of the Western world and is the scene of three top annual tournaments — the National Senior Hardcourt Championships in May and December and the Pacific Coast Men's Doubles Championships in March.

With its charming duck pond, stately Washington palms, romantic archways and perennial profusion of flowers, the Beach and Tennis Club continues to thrive as the social and family heart of now third and fourth generation La Jollans.

Under the Stars

Lights awaken on Prospect Street as the evening sun bathes La Jolla in spectacular pinks and golds. As dusk falls, the streets throb with the lively beat of strollers and window shoppers. Some savor superb cuisine in elegant settings while others linger in conversation by a piano, experiencing a favorite vintage. Classic cars or chauffered limousines transport La Jollans to·the theater, symphony, comedy showcase, gallery opening or one of the many festivities that raise funds for causes large and small. Whether decked out in top hat and tails for an annual gala or in a fifties poodle skirt for a friend's "Happy Fortieth," La Jollans enjoy an infinite variety of evening entertainment choices.

Index/Directory

About the...

Author

Gloria Andújar has lived in La Jolla since 1982. A native of Cuba, she was raised and educated in New York where she pursued a fast-paced career in international publishing. Gloria and her husband Julio combine many years of editorial and marketing expertise to provide publishing and consulting services through their own La Jolla-based company, Andújar Communication Technologies.

Photographer

A native of San Antonio, Texas, Jeremiah Sullivan has made San Diego his home since 1972. As a Scripps-trained marine biologist and underwater photographer, he has traveled to remote corners of the world on special assignments for *National Geographic*, *Travel & Leisure*, *LIFE* and *GEO*. Sullivan operates a studio in downtown San Diego where he provides commercial photography for leading national ad agencies and publishers.